TUG *of* WAR

TUG *of* WAR

DANIEL SULLIVAN JR.

Rev. date: 02/21/2018

To order additional copies of this book, contact:
Xlibris
1-888-795-4274
www.Xlibris.com
Orders@Xlibris.com
773042

CONTENTS

In everything, give thanks!

I give thanks always to my God and my Savior, the Lord Jesus Christ. Your unselfish love and long-suffering has always been displayed toward me even when I chose the wrong path. I was never left alone.

To my mother, Barbara Sullivan, and late father, Daniel Sullivan Sr., "they that sow in tears shall reap in joy!" Let the reaping begin! DeOnte', I pray the words from these pages attach themselves to your heart and provide you with the motivation needed to conquer daily wars. BreAna and Jeffery, continue to pull away from people, places, and things designed to hinder you from achieving success. Veronica, Talvin, and Melba, you all were on the inside, looking out. Thanks for the support on the inside. Now the results are out. Elainna, Travius, Teanna, Tia, Temperance, Imri, and Elon (the seed royal, 2 Kings 11:1 KJV), never be influenced by the negative, but use it as a stepping-stone to your dreams. Elise, Emani, and J'Michael, keep digging and pulling for maximum results in your pursuit for greatness.

Finally, to my circumstances, faults, and failures, I embrace your existence. You have inspired me to pursue hard after my purpose!

Wars are won by individuals who consistently conquer themselves!

—Daniel Sullivan Jr.

INTRODUCTION

THE GAME TUG-OF-WAR has been recognized as one of the most competitive sports known to man. A game of strength, stamina, and persistence, it is the ultimate test of one's will. Those who choose to involve themselves in this sport cannot begin in doubt, fear, or incompetence. There are certain dangers associated with this war if an individual is not physically, mentally, or emotionally prepared. In order to ensure the safety of the individuals, the rules and regulations are reviewed before the game commences.

The war always starts with the Captain, who is chosen by his or her peers. The Captain then carefully scans available individuals who he or she believes will be instrumental in leading their team to victory. The team members are strategically placed where the Captain deems necessary. The placement of each individual is determined by his or her strengths and weaknesses. A major component in the selection process is the Captain being able to recognize the potential of each team member chosen. Out of all the positions chosen, there is one that stands as top priority—the anchor or last one at the end of the rope. The anchor is allowed to dig deep into the foundation to secure his or her team's fate.

After the team selections have been completed and the rules have been thoroughly reviewed, the game or war is officially on. The team members get into their designated positions, which were chosen by the Captains, and wait for the queue or whistle to signify the start. The determining factor in victory would be the team that allows the other team to be pulled more than one yard out of their original position. The object of this game is to secure your position and never give up. When the team grows weary, there remains hope because the anchor accepts the weaknesses of his or her fellow team members.

Tug-of-war moves parallel with our lives. The game gives us an illustration of how we all have different wars, but our goals remain the same—to be victorious or successful. The worst thing that can happen in this game is for someone to give up. To give up is to accept defeat, and to accept defeat is to fail those connected to you.

CHAPTER 1

The Captain's Choice

O N THE PLAYGROUND is where freedom exists. No tests, no homework, no chalkboards, and no assignments. It is the most peaceful place that allows you to be yourself without being judged or called upon. The most influential person on the playground is always the captain. Whether it be basketball, relays, jump ropes, or Hula-Hoops, there is always a captain around to get everything started. Individuals start to gather around, readily available for the task ahead. Leaders or captains have been known to start by choosing the most talented individuals then moving to the least talented. The problem with that is, sometimes the most talented do not possess the character to pull the team through the toughest of times. Talent is a great thing to be chosen for, but without character, talent carries no weight.

The anchors have to be carefully selected because they must be able to carry the weaknesses of their team members. The anchor has to exhibit stability in all situations. That's why the captain's choice is so crucial to obtaining victory over any giant of an opponent.

The atmosphere is ignited with high expectations for both teams, but there is a slight dilemma. The captain delays the start. Team members get upset because of the delay, but they never stop to realize something has happened to the rope. After the slight delay is resolved, the competition begins. The whistle blows to signify the start, and the teams begin the battle.

Between the teams, there is an intense display of willpower. Positions, postures, and priorities are like revolving doors among the team members. Strengths and weaknesses are constantly exchanged. Weariness attempts to become the leader of each team, but encouragement from the captain keeps the teams elevated above their circumstances. When heads are held low and the physical body seems to appear numb from the pulling to and fro, there arises inner strength unknown to each team member. The battle is growing into a strenuous event that has pushed both teams to their maximum capacity. Total effort among many is the only strategy that needs to exist presently and throughout the event.

The tug-of-war competition exists on the playground, but from the playground to the playing field of life, we are still experiencing the effects of the tug-of-war. The playing field of life is on earth, where the war exists, but there is also an atmosphere around us that contains elements of war. We awake each day to face the same struggle or a different struggle according to how victorious we were in the previous struggle. Each struggle or war will consist of various levels, so to become victorious, every level has to be conquered. The techniques used in obtaining victory will be similar, but the approaches will be slightly different because of the nature of the team. The team members that exist in the tug-of-war are all physical in nature, but the team members in the game of life are physical and invisible. These two natures will be discussed more in chapter 2. Even the captains differ and have different functions in each tug-of-war.

The difference between the captain in the game tug-of-war and the Captain in life's tug-of-war is how individuals are chosen to participate. In the game of tug-of-war, individuals are chosen according to talents and gifts; but in the tug-of-war of life, every individual is chosen regardless of talents and gifts. The game has human beings as captains, who make decisions and position placements based on human knowledge. Life contains a Captain who has already predestined each individual for proper positioning based upon His purpose and will.

Sometimes when the playground captain chooses, there are mistakes in team selection because of his or her inability to perceive potential over problems. The Captain in the playing field of life makes no mistakes because He knows each individual and does not make His selections based on their imperfections or problems. When individuals recognize they have been chosen based on potential rather than problems, he or she exhibits a greater appreciation for the Captain and the tug-of-war.

On the playground, a list of problems, faults, and failures exist. The team members have records and files filled with achievements, accomplishments, awards, and recognition. These supporting documents are used among playground captains and leaders to determine how strong or weak the team may be or become. Trophies and crowns made of material are given to playground winners, but the winners in the playing field of life receive incorruptible crowns that never fade away.

CHAPTER 2

Realize It's a War!

THE CRITICISM THAT individuals express toward those involved in a tug-of-war is one based upon prejudgments or biased opinions. The ability to see the struggle of each individual and the purpose that the struggle serves can only be perceived by individuals who have experienced wars themselves. In the beginning of the war, each team member maintains a fresh glow of excitement on his or her countenance. The glow that is being radiated in the atmosphere draws many onlookers and gainsayers.

Sometimes, the captain casts forth his or her confidence in the look or appearance of the team. Some war participants make careless errors due to their focus on looks and appearance, better known as matter. When the focus on the war is shifted from war to matter, then the ability to recognize there is a war rarely exists.

Matter is a physical body or substance that occupies space according to its mass. The focal shift on the matter within the tug-of-war causes an individual or team to base decisions on what exists in front of them. The dilemma that confronts this decision-making process can grow into an erratic whirlwind of indecisiveness. The intention of the war, although physical beings are involved, was never intended for matter to become the center of attention. The physical side of war does exist, but the elements of war align themselves with the physical to cause a greater influence toward victory or defeat. Too much focus on matter will weaken one's ability to overcome the pulling and tugging of the war.

When given ample time, matter eventually breaks down and crumbles under pressure and strain. The results of matter breaking down will be visibly recognized in one's demeanor. Attitudes reflect leadership, so when matter is allowed to become the leader, it dictates every decision made within the war. Every emotion is ignited and driven by physical factors, such as style, recognition, beauty, body sculpture; and don't forget, size does matter! These factors are used to gauge one's performance or stamina in the war, so the pressure for the participant to maintain the matter becomes his or her priority.

Restoring the proper alignment of priorities can become a very challenging task to someone who has placed so much matter in the forefront. Individual positioning is affected while the ability to see becomes limited. Being improperly positioned causes thought patterns to become congested and to not be processed properly. The processing of these thoughts cannot be accomplished through material means, but they have to be arranged and captivated by the elements of war.

The key purpose of the elements is to dictate what takes place in the atmosphere. Elements are one of four substances—earth, air, water, or fire. These substances usually cause changes in the atmosphere that result in changes in the physical performance of an individual. For example, if a fire breaks out in a farmland, the physical labor of production will be greatly affected. If there is inclement weather, it can affect one's physical ability to operate a motor vehicle. When the air contains humidity or has an extreme heat index, it affects one's physical ability to work outside. The earth embraces each substance but is affected by universal influence. The sun stands outside the earth, but it can control the physical activities that take place on the earth.

A summary of this brief science project is, we, as physical beings, are always affected by the elements in the atmosphere, although we reside on the earth. The tug-of-war that exists did not start with the physical war on the playground, but it started in the atmosphere above. Just like the sun has its effects on things on the earth, there exists another Son that influences changes in the atmosphere as well as on the earth. An individual trying to change the purpose of the sun is a complete waste because when it's hot or cold outside, there remains but one choice— deal with it!

The same principle applies to the Son. When your situation is getting a little overwhelming due to the purpose of the Son, there remains one choice—deal with it! Too many individuals are trying to change the Son's purpose and waking up in the same situation. The best way to deal with any situation that the sun or Son places you in is to realize the reality, embrace its purpose, and respond positively. When the embracing moment takes place, there comes a change in positioning. The matter surrenders to the Son and makes itself available for the Son's use in the war.

"To everything there is a season, and a time to every purpose under the heaven" (Ecclesiastes 3:1). This is the turning point of the war, because the recognition of the war's purpose has been embraced and the matter has been dethroned as the leader of the war. After one realizes there's a war at hand, one's thoughts are elevated above the circumstances, and the Son becomes the leader over the matter. The Son becoming the leader causes our thoughts to be organized and to flow in sync with the Son's purpose. The organization of our thoughts causes us to meditate on positive things, which will result in positive speaking, producing positive results.

The consistent acceptance of this season will produce multiple victories in other seasons of war. There will be a greater understanding of "a time to love, and a time to hate; a time of war, and a time of peace" (Ecclesiastes 3:8). Positive thinking will guide us through many wars and will lead us into a land of peace. Once we enter the land of peace, we can take a look back at the war and rejoice in the fact that it took the war to gain the peace. The most victorious individuals are able to live successfully and conquer many wars because they obtain peace right in the middle of the war. The atmosphere is ignited by elements such as finances, relationships, temptations, lust, greed, and power; but the conqueror maintains a state of peacefulness in the midst of this season.

The benefits of realizing it's a war are the support, the backing of the Son, and the confidence in knowing that when matter fails, the Son never fails. Realizing it's a war also influences our motives during the war. Why we are fighting the way we fight has a meaning. Who we choose to fight with and for is greatly determined by the realization of the war. What we are trying to gain from the war, how we enter the war, which tools we fight with, and when we choose to fight are all questions to be addressed by our motives. Ultimately, the war's length and outcome are solely based our ability to respond properly when faced with the most difficult challenges.

When there has been a victory in one area of the war, there has to be a greater awareness for the wars ahead. The wars only intensify to develop the individual and draw him or her closer to the Son. The distance between the individual and the Son must be reduced to a relationship that results in victorious living.

CHAPTER 3

The Anchor

A S THE WAR intensifies, much energy is expended; therefore, a sense of security would be in high demand. Anytime a certain amount of energy is used up, individuals can become vulnerable. When this stage occurs in the tug-of-war, whether in life or in the game, the team members must feel security or get the notion that "someone has our back!" Having the confidence in an individual takes a lot of courage in vulnerable times.

A lot of people hardly ever come to a place of security because they can never bring themselves to trust anyone in their most vulnerable times. They are afraid of being disappointed, abused, mistreated, walked over, backstabbed, or even talked about. Unfortunately, those individuals never experience true victory in the tug-of-war. They tend to think they have advanced due to the fact that they have moved forward a little in the war, but the misleading factor is, forward movement does not always represent victory. In a movement, things appear to be more organized; but without specific disciplines, the appearance soon fades away, and what lies beneath could rise up into chaos. True victory in the most vulnerable times comes with forward progress, which is represented by the individual's growth, development, and level of maturity. This level is called the maturation process.

The maturation process of an individual involves vulnerability and open-mindedness. There will be various sources of strengths, dependencies, and reliabilities removed in this process. A decaying away of friends, family, co-workers, and leaders will begin to take place, like the transformation from having baby teeth to adult teeth. The teething process starts in growth, development, detachment, exposure, alignment, and realignment. All stages have to be completed before full growth takes place. And the growth has to be maintained with proper discipline, or the time it takes to lose what you have gained is swift.

Teeth are held in place by their roots or, in this case, their Anchors. Many patients hate root canals because the root canals can be very painful. There has to be drilling, cleaning, filling, and crowning to complete the process. Afterward, restoration takes place. Within the tug-of-war, these similar processes will take place.

The stages of maturation vary according to each person. In some instances, there must be extensive drilling before cleaning, filling, and crowning. If there was an option to be crowned and to escape the root canal, then life would be like the nap of an infant—peaceful and full of wonderful thoughts and dreams. Many people choose to live their lives constantly trying to avoid the root canal. They continue to cover up the decay with crowns, which represent achievements, rewards, cars, homes, family, leadership, bodily exercises, and church. All these crowns will quickly vanish because of what lies beneath.

The pain associated with this process usually leaves one drained and with a loss of energy. When energy levels have been depleted and all hope seems to be gone, an ounce of trust must remain. That ounce of trust must be issued to someone designated to be the Anchor. The vulnerabilities have to be connected to the Anchor because when the war is spinning out of control, there has to be stability. At this moment in time, the Anchor has taken full responsibility for the team.

The choosing of the Anchor has its rewards and consequences. If the wrong Anchor is chosen, this could mean defeat for any individual or team because the Anchor must stand firm on a solid foundation. An Anchor chosen without a good foundation is a disaster waiting to happen. In most tug-of-war games, the Anchor is in the back to pull the weight of the team and secure their positions. If the Anchor does not have a firm grip or is not planted properly, he or she would lose the ability to maintain absolute control.

An out-of-control Anchor not only leaves the individual vulnerable but also exposes the whole team to defeat. There are various styles of anchors, but they all have the same function. That primary function is to hold things in place or to secure positioning.

In life, sometimes our situations seem to have us twirling out of control with finances, relationships, temptations, careers, education, and family; but all can be brought under control with the proper Anchor. In the playing field of life, there comes a time when you arrive at your wit's end and the end of the rope is near. This time is very crucial and destiny driven because the decisions made in this moment can pull you forward into chaotic turmoil or pull you back into purpose.

Some people think the pulling forward is the positive aspect in this tug-of-war, but that should be carefully considered. When the tug-of-war event is taking place, the team being pulled forward is in danger of the crossover. The crossover represents the place where the exchange takes place from victory to defeat. It also causes a directional shift in one's focal agenda. The removal of an individual from his or her original position, which was established for success, and the detouring of their focus toward the decoy for success is quite powerful yet subtle. This crossover process is designed to redirect your path and change your destination. The Captain predestines everyone; therefore, the challenge is for each member to stay in the proper position to fulfill his or her purpose and destiny.

It's okay to be on the edge or even at your wit's end, but letting go and giving up pulls you over to the side of defeat, which ultimately leads to the loss of identity. This loss of identity will have you in a state of confusion, forgetting what team you were initially chosen for. The results will start to manifest in your thoughts first, then it will be sown into your heart. Afterwards, what you think becomes what you speak—defeated!

Negativity becomes apparel that you drape yourself with daily while strolling through the streets of defeatism. Along these streets, hitchhikers such as fear, doubt, gossip, complaint, bitterness, anxiety, discouragement, and hopelessness await to become passengers riding shotgun on this downhill journey. These travelers serve no other purpose than to impede your progress and cause you to exit before you reach the determined destination. When the wrong path is taken, the journey to your destination becomes lengthy and exhaustive. The travel time in minutes turn into hours, the hours turn into days, the days turn into months, and the months turn into years.

Our testimony becomes "If I had done this or that, then I could have accomplished this or that." Well, this or that is what we have become, and the only way to change that is to conquer this, the tug-of-war. When choosing who or what we decide to become, our Anchor lies in the balance, and destiny awaits our decision.

The pressure of choosing the Anchor in these trying times becomes strenuous, but the only way to maintain insight on the proper Anchor is to know what the purpose of the anchor is. Discovering your purpose opens the door to discovering the Anchor's purpose.

CHAPTER 4

Weak-ness

THE PROCESS OF discovering, recognizing, realizing, and choosing can be a grueling task. The effects of the war start to take a toll on the mental, emotional, and physical capabilities of the individual. These three areas have to be consistently maintained in order for an individual to operate in full capacity. The atmospheric shifts and changes can play an instrumental part in the balancing act required to stay focused during the tug-of-war. There must be a willingness to keep the mental, emotional, and physical arenas protected. Allowing any of these areas to go lacking places you and those connected to you in a vulnerable position also. The natural tendency for energy to get low during the war is expected, but maintaining a balance can be very challenging. Persistence, patience, and practice have to be introduced to our mind, soul, and body, even when the war enters its most intense moments.

Things that engage the mind—such as thoughts, words, beliefs, and imaginations—affect our mental capacity. The mind is, foremost, a target that is aimed at to alter the participant's perception of the end result. If an individual starts believing that he or she can win and the mind is altered during the war by the elements that exist in the atmosphere, the individual will lose heart in the midst of the war. The once-victorious belief system will be overshadowed with doubt and fear.

That's why it is of utmost importance before, during, and after the war that we shun profane and vain babblings (2 Timothy 2:16), which can cause us to err in our process. When the mind has been infested with babblings and negativity, it starts to affect our emotional state. What we hear, see, and meditate on become what we believe. Once the belief is confirmed, our lifestyle or style of life is conformed.

Individuals are constantly shouting instructions, some in your favor and some against you. All these shouts are surrounding the tug-of-war. There has to exist the ability or skill to separate what and who is for you or against you. Our mental focus has to be fortified by our belief system, which has to be constructed with positive thoughts and influences. Even the images that we gaze upon or the television that we view affects what we believe. Don't take this for granted.

If we constantly witness defeat, negativity, cheating, abuse, unfaithfulness, or violence, our style of life will reflect what we witnessed. It takes a moment for the seed to be planted in our heart or to be sown into our emotions, but eventually, it will manifest. Flowers don't bloom overnight; it takes time and process. There are certain things that must take place in the atmosphere to influence the manifestation of what has been planted. Seeds don't grow in places where they cannot take root; therefore, it is important for us, as participants in this war, to constantly monitor what gets into our hearts or emotional arenas.

The emotional arena, or heart area, is most sensitive under intense war. The sensitivity causes our heart or emotions to become a seedbed for our thoughts to lodge in. Once the thoughts enter the seedbed, they lie dormant, awaiting the fertilization process to take place. The process of fertilization takes place whenever we consistently entertain thoughts that are linked to the one that has entered the seedbed.

The entertainment industry demonstrates this process in various ways. The most successful actors have to be professional entertainers, consistently meditating on what is written or read. Everything that is written or read becomes what he or she acts. This acting can only be successful when what has entered the heart manifests. When we watch a movie, we are only watching what transpired in the mental arena first—thoughts, imaginations, words, and beliefs. The characters are developed in the mental arena first and then meditated upon until they come to life in the heart of the writer. The writer then begins to write out of the seedbed of the heart or emotions to produce the physical form of what is written. That's why it's important for the reader or viewer to be careful of what is meditated upon because whatever or whoever influences the writer will influence the reader or viewer.

It seems a bit trivial to dig that deep for answers regarding the style of life we choose to live, but our defeat in this war can be so quick and subtle if we don't maintain a sharp awareness of the elements of war. We must be careful and stay on guard against thoughts that attempt to sway us from our destiny. We can recognize those thoughts easily because they only appear when we choose to move forward by pulling back from negative influences within people, places, or things.

The physical arena stands as the last representative to secure our position and safeguard our energy depletion. Energy levels start high at the beginning of the war and must be replenished during the activities transpiring within the war. If the energy level falls below the required threshold, the individual will be in danger of entering a state of weakness.

The mental and emotional arenas have a direct affect on the physical arena because they process the information necessary for the physical to withstand the pressures and challenges of life. The tug-of-war is filled with pitfalls and elevated stress levels that can break the physical abilities of the participants down. The combination of high demands and adhering to rules and regulations will ultimately lead to one trying to juggle priorities and commitments. The juggling act involves discovering different personalities, and while the personalities reveal themselves, there are choices to make regarding which personality to connect with. Our perception of who is for us and who is against us needs to remain clear.

Whenever we enter the war, there is a tendency to join ourselves physically with individuals whose sole purpose is to withdraw strength from us. To protect ourselves from these individuals, the mental and emotional arenas have to be kept in balance. Anytime our abilities in these arenas fall short, the physical is unable to recognize the difference between the depositors and withdrawers.

The banking system gives us a prime example of how to recognize the depositor and withdrawer. Individuals who qualify for withdrawals have already made an investment or deposit into their account. They have already planted seeds that will produce significant growth in due time. The work habits of the depositor are consistent with his or her account standing. The account would represent the individual's style of life because when the lifestyle is developed, then the account grows. The participant who tries to establish an account with nothing to deposit will always attempt to withdraw from that account, expecting something for nothing. This individual will always maintain little strength or negative balances due to their unwillingness to discipline themselves in the midst of the war.

There is the possibility for a depositor and withdrawer to exist in your life, but both work together for your good. The purpose of the deposit is to have something to withdraw from. The depositor makes constant deposits to secure the future and establish a solid foundation to build that future upon. The withdrawals are made to assist the depositor in maintaining a structured lifestyle or style of life in which he or she becomes beneficial to those in their circle of influence.

The tragedy that takes place within the war is when we are unable to distinguish between the purpose of the depositor, who is qualified to withdraw, and the withdrawer, who never deposits but attempts to make withdrawals from a negative balance. The strength that remains in all us during this grueling war has to be protected and inaccessible to individuals who only want to withdraw strength for his or her benefit. They never attempt to replenish what has been taken, nor do they attempt to assist you in your weakest moment.

When the physical body gets weak, it requires certain sources to regain strength. There are always substitutes that are offered in the replenishing phase. They appear to be the real source, have similar ingredients, and come packaged in similar packaging; but when the small print is read, there might be one essential ingredient missing. This missing ingredient stands as the one thing that makes all other ingredients come together to benefit us as participants in this tug-of-war. We might feel strength temporarily, but we are unable to withstand the pressures that constantly come with the war. When this process takes place, we are in danger of being weak, and the most dangerous thing is to fall into weakness or the state of being weak. The state represents a persistent pattern designed to keep the mind in a stagnant position. This condition ushers defeat into our lives and attempts to show us flash cards filled with failures and hopeless situations.

When we become weak, we are unable to withstand certain pressures and sustain and carry heavy loads or strains. If we fail to connect to the destined physical attachments, there only remains opportunity for defeat. Weakness can be overcome, but every arena has to be reestablished and brought into balance. The attempt to repair one arena and leave the others to stand alone only leads us into deception; this will eventually lead us into a circle of defeat, which is difficult to break.

CHAPTER 5

Pride's Invasion

ONE OF THE major goals in a tug-of-war is to secure a reasonable territory or establish a solid foundation which we can depend on when strength is weak. The difficulty that exists when trying to secure our territory is accomplishing it while under extreme hardship. The ability to bring the mental, emotional, and physical in alignment will secure our territory and establish a solid foundation. Oftentimes, we falter in the assumption that everything is okay when we regain a little strength. Our confidence is elevated, and the light at the end of the tunnel has appeared. Slowly, we start to rebuild areas that have been torn down and destroyed. While this process is taking place, opposition must come to hinder the progression. We strategize to gather those things that were lost in the war and fight to maintain our positions of recovery. After the struggle to bring order to the turmoil that has broken loose in our lives, we have to be prepared for a hostile invasion or takeover.

There is an adversary that exists in our atmosphere that desires to take control of the destined direction of our purpose. This adversary hovers above us like the extraterrestrial beings awaiting an invitation to land and occupy the available territories. The practice of maintaining mental focus and digesting positive substances will assist in the withstanding of this phenomenal force. Rejoicing over one area conquered and leaving others undone only causes us to vacate the home front temporarily. Sometimes, it takes years of sweat and tears to triumph over the pitfalls of life, but in a matter of seconds, this triumph can be transformed into defeat. We must carefully evaluate our lives and constantly look in the mirror to locate any flaws that can turn into future failures. Every morning, we are given an opportunity to examine ourselves and become the judge and jury before our day begins. Some might say that a mirror doesn't exist in their atmosphere, but if the mirror doesn't exist, there are face-to-face moments each day. We stand in front of people every day and have the chance to ask them what they see in us.

There is a plot being laid out by the adversary every moment of our lives. It is designed to fracture or bring disturbance to the things that strengthen our relationship with the Captain. Daily self-evaluations keep the proper mixture of the combined ingredients that will fortify our relationship with the Captain. The plot by the adversary has one mission, and that is to destroy relationships. To execute the plans accurately, the adversary has to make plans to invade your establishment or relationship. The invasion process is very strategic and has to be organized by dedicated, skillful leadership. The invasion will have a direct effect on an individual's reaction to the situation because it scatters the thought process.

The success of this plan solely depends upon the individual's unwillingness to judge oneself. When the judgment process is delayed or denied, it leaves a portal open through which the adversary can infiltrate and start to conquer small territories of our lives. The adversary does not perform this plan alone but has an army of influences that have submitted themselves to the order of their leader. They demonstrate the teamwork model, which should be exemplified in the successful lifestyle but is instead modeled for destruction. The plan is so carefully organized and detailed for maximum effectiveness. It is always being conspired while we are in repair mode or in the reorganization phase.

The adversary's invasion process is provided with ammunition directly sponsored by our emotions. How we feel about what we are dealing with, how we view the war, what we think about the Captain, what we think about our fellow team members, why we have to go through this, who cares about us, who else is going through this like us, when this war will end, when our turn to succeed is, and where we find answers or escape routes are all questions fueled by our emotions. These questions always lead to curiosity, and when our curiosities are not fulfilled, doubts enter. The purpose of doubt is to make you think that the progress you have experienced was never worth it and all the hard work and dedication that has been demonstrated in the organizational phase was wasteful. As soon as these thoughts dominate our mind, an opening appears for the invasion to take place. This is the portal through which our adversary loves to travel because it allows free flow and frequent visits.

Well, let's take a look at this unknown masked adversary. It goes by the name of pride and is very popular among its peers. The beginning stages of pride usually start within individuals who have allowed their esteem level to be depleted. These depletions take place when we look for appreciation and value from others, like various leaders or captains who enter our lives.

This process begins at childhood and remains with us until our departure from this earth, not the war. As little children, we are lifted up when we are appreciated and given value by our parents or peers. It is a natural building process to our character and future endeavors. That's why parents, leaders, guardians, and teachers are compelled to speak positively to children while there are young because this motivates them to achieve greater things in life. The more positive vibes a child receives, the more vibes are returned to others along the pathway of life. The signs of pride can always be traced back to childhood. Children who feel less appreciated or feel devalued tend to grow into adults who have the same makeup. The recognition of this important missing link will cause an adult to change his or her ways and seek help to become less dependent upon people and more dependent upon his or her Captain.

Appreciation and value are stimulants to the human psyche, and the lack thereof causes us to swoop into a self-destructive dependency mode. We all tend to lean toward individuals who add to our emotional makeup because it strengthens our ability to stand in tough situations. The fallacy that eventually appears in our lives is when we lift those same individuals up on pedestals and begin to worship them for the influence that they have on us, whether it be good or bad. We can also fall into traps set by ourselves because of how we think and feel about ourselves or our complete individuality. To receive appreciation and value is not negative unless we become solely dependent upon it to achieve our potential. When we strive to achieve our potential based on our dependency of appreciation and value, everything that we set out to accomplish is influenced by others' opinions and approvals. This is an accident waiting to happen and eventually does happen. It's only a matter of time and changing of seasons.

Our hopes and dreams are spun into a web of deception when we worship others' opinions and approvals regarding us as individuals. To escape this web of deception takes self-confidence in one's own ability dispersed by the Captain, because self-confidence without proper attachments will lead us into self-exaltation. We spend tons of energy and exhaust time attempting to build our reputations and images. The definition of who we are stems from the material things accumulated over time rather than learning our true identity through a personal relationship with our Captain.

Within this war, there will come a time to decide whom we are pulling for and how long we will be pulling. When this time comes, it is very important that our relationship with our Captain is fully engaged. Through this relationship with our Captain, we gain confidence in the Captain and not ourselves, because our dependency rests on the Captain and not in ourselves. The Captain's role in disassembling the invasion is very important and can determine the destiny of the participant.

The overwhelming onslaught of pride affects the mental faculties, causing us to cease grasping for positive reinforcement. Ultimately, the pride invasion begins to decrease our ability to recover from such a devastating takeover. Without positive reinforcement, we become filled with selfish desires and impure motives. Every reaction is based on what matters to us, and regardless of whom we affect, the bottom line is our satisfaction. At the end of the day, it's about our emotions, feelings, efforts, and accomplishments.

The mixture of self-confidence and overzealousness becomes a potent component for a disaster waiting to happen. The only way to dilute this deadly mixture is to add a large portion of humility, which causes the solution to materialize into brokenness. Positive reinforcement will appear through the act of submission and moments of humility. This process will open up the emotional passageways that have been blocked by pounds of pride. Usually, when the passageways are open, individuals start to enter our lives to detour us and cause the passageways to be congested with thoughts of remaining in the same state or season. When we allow humility to enter our lives, we become vulnerable to the onslaught of pride because we have to now rely on someone or something for guidance.

To be continued...

CHAPTER 6

The Substitution

D URING THE WAR, there comes a time when we cannot fulfill our obligations due to lack of strength, encouragement, or willpower. In this moment, crucial decisions have to be made by the individual, captain, or Captain. There must be an assessment of characteristics and personalities during this decision-making process. As the war intensifies, individuals become fearful and tend to retreat when they feel the war has gotten out of control. When this atmosphere exists, there are others who have been handpicked by the captain or the Captain. The other individuals have been awaiting the moment to enter the war for only two reasons: to build or to destroy.

These individuals waiting are known as replacements or substitutions and are destined to enter our lives unawares. Their purposes have been predestined, and the only way to determine who has come to build or destroy in our moment of weakness is to consult with the Captain. The insight and perception of the Captain looks beyond the physical form of the individual and digs deep into the intent of the individual.

In the sporting world, there are constant substitutions made to execute certain agendas. Most substitutions are only temporary, when the main participant is unable to perform due to his or her inabilities. That's why in chapter 1, the emphasis is placed on the proper choosing of Captains, because if there is discrepancy made in the choosing of Captains or leaders, then the substitution can hinder our process. Organizations have to be careful when sitting down to discuss who will be the Captain or leader of their team because the direction of that team will lie in the hands of the Captain. When a captain has evil intentions, the substitutions are made to hinder our performance and discourage our reentry to the war or game. On the other hand, when the Captain has pure motives, the substitutions are made to assist in our victory and to give us a moment to recover. In the recovery mode, we are given time to regain our strength and get a clear perspective on the breakdown of the war.

In a hospital room, when a patient is in recovery, it is a very serious moment. The doctors have certain assignments in what type of prescriptions to administer to the patients. The nursing staff has to carefully fulfill their duties while trying to carry out the doctor's (leader's or Captain's) assignment. The length of recovery will depend upon the reaction of the patient's body, the administration of prescriptions, the experience of the staff, and the perception or diagnosis of the doctor. Recovery rooms or periods have a major impact on the future of the patient and play an important role in the strengthening procedure required to fulfill that patient's purpose in life. That's why the visitors that are allowed are limited and special precautions are taken to eliminate any germs or contaminants from entering the recovery room.

Recovery rooms are mostly located near the operating rooms so you can have a smooth transition after surgery. Usually, the first stages of recovery are painful because the body has to adjust to the strain and stress of surgery. There has been constant cutting, pulling, tearing, removing, shaving, peeling, sewing, mending, and bleeding. Throughout these various *ings*, there is always movement going on. This constant movement causes the body to be weary and to experience slight discomfort in some areas. During the majority or all the surgical processes, the patient is usually unaware or unconscious from anesthesia.

Anesthesia is used to sedate the patient so that the experience during the surgical process will be painless and acceptable. It places the patient in a total state of unawareness and is very beneficial for the recovery process. The only thing that can happen negatively when anesthesia is administered is the patient being unable to regain consciousness. This becomes a tremendous intimidation for the patient and moves them to become reluctant to receive this method. Unfortunately, no matter how much an individual fears the method, certain conditions deny the patient any input in the decision-making process.

Some situations are so intense and damaging to our physical body that they call for extreme action and radical change. This is where the Captain, captains, leaders, or guardians come into play. The decision can never be about what the individual might want but always has to be about what the individual may need to survive such a traumatic experience. Since we are unaware and unable to comprehend the seriousness of the situation, we are left in the hands of those who should be capable of affecting our recovery. Life or death awaits us.

Once the necessary precautions are taken and the procedures have been performed properly, then we are set to reenter the war. We have to carefully evaluate our next move once we re-enter the war and consider the obstacles as stepping-stones instead of stumbling blocks. Grasping tidbits of information involved in the previous process will expedite our transformation and influence our growth and development for the next war to come. With great assurance, there will be another war, and whether we remain stable or allow substitutes to enter as they please will be a choice for us to make.

The substitution process involves many components that are designed to elevate our ability to perform under pressure. Our opposition consistently challenges our input as a team member. Every move has to be calculated carefully, and every motive must be constantly scanned for reasons. When our motives are established, then we are able to proceed with the decision-making process.

The substitution plays a major role in our transition from being inactive to producing positive results, so it's very important that we get an understanding, while we are inactive, of what our role is and will be upon reentry to the war. We should not spend our inactive moments engaging in unproductive and wasteful people, places, or things. Every season of the war will call for desperate measures sometimes, and when these times arrive, we must be prepared to make radical decisions. Although these decisions will be radical, they can also be detrimental to our ability to overcome if our thoughts are crowded with ideas derived from unreliable sources. Refer to "Chapter 4: Weakness."

Now that the substitution has been made and the process of reentry to the war has begun, our original position might be shifted, so we have to be ready to adjust to the realignment. This shift will be discomforting because of our ideologies, which have been built on what is comfortable to the self. Well, the systematic lifestyle that dictated comfort levels for us has to be reconsidered because change has come and change is necessary for growth and progress. When we refuse to change and move forward, whether in another position or the same, the substitution that will come for our relief becomes our resolve. It is a very discouraging moment when we have to sit aside and gaze upon another with higher hopes, greater vision, security, and a willingness to conform to the renewing of the mind.

Most individuals hang their heads in defeat when substitutions take place, but there is no need to view this as defeat. When this event takes place, our perception is the one thing that orchestrates our comeback or recovery. When we come to terms with ourselves and realize our shortcomings and the reason or motive behind them, then we will be able to launch a new vision for our lives. Within this war, we will suffer loss; but to maintain a level of sanity, there has to be the acceptance and release of the loss. This loss has to be perceived as a gain to us, or the thought patterns will become negative and will usher us into utter defeat.

To perceive the loss as gain takes a lot of meditation and decipherment of every thought during the substitution process. Upon deciphering our thoughts and motives, we can realize the wrong turns, attachments, influences, and chosen captains that have brought our lives full circle. There always exists an underlying truth below the foundation of our loss—it is our decision-making or destiny. The bottom line is, we have a part to play and our input is necessary.

We tend to shy away from responsibility when hardship arrives and takes a quick tour of our downtown or downtime. During downtime, things move a little slowly, and sightseeing is a high priority. We have to be ever so careful when our lives become the target for tourism because onlookers and visitors will praise us for our history or ability to appear settled. This presents us with an outstanding opportunity for the onlookers to see the works of our Captain and not the work of the self. Humility has to be introduced as our tour guide while watchers wait in expectation for the reason why we survived or overcame. The self would love to take charge and display the handiwork of the Captain, only to receive accolades for personal gratification.

Humility is the only tour guide we need for hardship to pass through downtown or downtime without causing such devastation or destruction to our infrastructure. The impact of humility during the war is hinged on how we feel about what others are thinking of us, because sometimes humility portrays an individual as weak and helpless. So to rebut the incoming opinions and perfectionists, we tend to stand tall with the appearance of victory when, on the inside, our self has defeated us.

One thing about the self is walking and appearing as if we are strong or that we got it altogether feeds the pride seed that lies within us. The longer the seed is fed and nourished with lies and deceit, the more powerful it becomes. Pride slowly eats away at our destiny and purpose in the war and tries to thwart the plan of the Captain. When this disturbing activity is allowed to carry on unchecked or is not brought under subjection, it deteriorates our relationship with the Captain and fellow team members.

The Captain has predetermined our positions before the war, and when the substitutions are brought in and not received properly by our humility, there stands a great chance that a fall is inevitable. We have to constantly stay in contact with the Captain, not captain, during the war because the escorting of pride into our ballroom of emotions will create an atmosphere that is ignited with self-exaltation and anonymous accolades.

CHAPTER 7

Spinning in the Crossroads

I F WE COULD incorporate robin-like characteristics in our situation, there would be constant communication to warn us of impending trouble. The bird known as the robin is friendly and helpful in times of trouble. They tend to make high-pitched noises when there is a threat to their habitation. The robin is also called a songbird, and the importance of having this characteristic is being able to sing in the midst of turmoil or to make a joyful noise. The other characteristic of the robin is its migratory habits. These habits can be its downfall because of instability. When robins tend to wander or rove, it can cause them to end up at the wrong destination.

Our surroundings, like the robins', influences our behavior. We can be friendly and helpful in times of trouble and also be able to express ourselves positively when in turmoil. These are all great ways to stay focused on where we are headed, but we can be detoured by our migratory habits. Our instabilities and indecisiveness can lead us into situations and wars that hinder our progressive movement.

The destinations in life that we come to are a sum total of the decisions we make. The constant pressure of what choice to make hovers over our minds, like satellites in space, transmitting information for movement and progress. When information is needed for a new level, technicians rely on satellite transmission to point them in the right direction. When there is a delay regarding information, panic and fear enter the hearts of leaders across the nation. The main fear is the one of not knowing what direction a country, nation, or community is headed toward or having an unknown destination.

There was a story about a man named Abram who was told to leave home and travel to an unknown place. There were no satellites available in those days, but there was something more powerful than the satellites—it was a voice. This was no ordinary voice; it was one of authority and guidance. There will come a time in this tug-of-war when satellite transmission will cease and information is delayed. There will be a hunger for direction and guidance, but this hunger will be mixed with fear and panic. This place is called the crossroads.

There are four significant directions at the crossroads. They are north, south, east, and west. Each direction contains a purpose but is not necessarily your ultimate purpose. Your purpose can only be discovered through your hearing and maintaining a sense of awareness. The transmission of information will come through several sources, but there has to be caution used in choosing the proper source. There are many sources pulling on your emotions from all directions, and the goal is to keep you in a state of confusion. The purpose of the state of confusion is to stop forward progress and ignite the inability to process thoughts properly. When this neutralization occurs, time becomes your enemy while you continue to struggle with choices about whether to cross the line or stay in the comfort zone. This is where an unstable mind-set occurs, and you become stuck in your ways.

An individual stuck in his or her ways constantly makes the statement "That's just the way I am and always have been" or "It is what it is." The only reason these statements exist is a lack of identity. When you never plug into your true purpose in life, there is a tendency to lose your identity in people, places, or things. The people that we hang around continue to design our lives based on our individual needs. The needs can come in the form of self-esteem, where we need praise and acceptance to satisfy our images. This void usually starts in childhood, where parents are mostly responsible for helping children recognize who they are and what their real purpose in life is. The only way that parents are able to secure a child's future and give them an awareness of their purpose is to know their own purpose. A leader without a purpose results in a follower without an identity. When parents are blinded by their own distractions and lack of understanding, it causes a communication breakdown in the parent-child relationship.

The breakdown that occurs is ultimately the foundation on which the new relationship is developed. This relationship has no trust or support system providing the security needed to engage in proper social skills. The result of this process will be a pulling away and misguidance, eventually causing indecisiveness.

Desperation has now become the driving force to validate the self. There is a reaching and pulling for individuals who somehow seem to ignite a sense of value and justification of who we are and are bound to become. These individuals become critical in shaping our belief system, which has been unstable. The tug-of-war now is great because we try to hold on to our foundational beliefs versus fictional beliefs. This tug causes us to spin in circles while trying to grasp the concept of a relationship. We now build relationships with individuals designed to steer us away from our true purpose. In the realist sense, many will not achieve their ultimate purpose due to their lives being built on fiction, not truth.

To avoid getting stuck in the spin of the crossroads, truth has to be confronted and embraced. It has to be a day-to-day, face-to-face encounter with the self, and we have to acknowledge imperfections that hinder the pursuit of purpose. How long will we run away from ourselves? There has to be an elimination of the finger-pointing and placing blame elsewhere. The person in the mirror we gaze upon daily before we leave home needs to be checked and held accountable. The brief moment in taking the selfie or snap should be a moment of truth. "Am I sending the real me out to the world or a phony copy of something I faked temporarily?" This question should be answered prior to pressing send. We are the only solution to our problem, and the only way to come out of the spin is to recognize that fixing this starts with "me."

CHAPTER 8

Draw Strength

I T'S OKAY TO depend on a team for strength, but possessing personal strength is a key factor to winning personal wars. The mistake we constantly make in our personal war is looking to others for strength instead of allowing ourselves to be strengthened from within. We figure that if we are around strong people, then we can endure the tug-of-war. Unfortunately, the issue with this is, when we are not surrounded by the strong, we become weak and crumble under the pressure of the war. The weakness within is never addressed before the surrounding of the strong, so we think it cannot be fixed through this method. But we later realize it's not the case. Let's not misunderstand. There is strength in numbers. Also, two are better than one. These are great factors that influence our victory within the tug of this war, but without our personal effort, these factors are null and void.

When a team is set to pull on the rope in the tug-of-war, each member should be utilizing personal strength, combined with corporate strength, to ensure victory. The process of the tug can be exhausting and challenging, but those that endure to the end will have the ultimate victory. If there is no investment in personal strength, eventually the evidence of it will be displayed during the most intense part of the war. Just when the team needs you the most, your weakness is displayed due to the image maintenance of strength and not the day-to-day personal effort to invest in "yourself."

The investment in the self is the most important investment we can make before attempting to invest in others. We often put ourselves on the back burner and allow others to draw strength from us when they have not invested the time to personally improve ourselves. When we allow others to withdraw from us what we don't have enough of, it places us in a state of defeat. It's very difficult to give something you barely possess and have enough remaining for yourself. Strength is something we need to make it to the end—as a matter of fact, just getting through any trial, persecution, test, hardship, etc.

In Luke 8:43-48, there was a woman (no name) who had an issue of bleeding for twelve years. She had spent all her living wages on physicians and could not be healed by any of them. Her issue placed her in a weak state, but before the issue, she must have made personal investments in herself, because her belief system was still strong. Individuals who don't take the time to invest in themselves usually possess a frail belief system. They end up turning to the wrong people, places, and things to get strength.

This woman without a name represents a person without an identity, combined with a consistent issue. The scripture states that "she spent all" on physicians, which means that material wealth or abundance may not be the answer for victory. I'm sure the cost of medical attention was expensive like it is today, but the difference is, she most likely didn't have insurance like today. Just for a second, think of the ramifications of not having the support of insurance like Medicaid or Medicare. All she had was coming from a place of not enough, but she managed to dig deep into her belief system and grab hold of something much more powerful than money—faith! The moment her faith connected with the source, she was immediately made whole. Being in a state of wholeness leaves one limitless and without void.

In order to draw strength, there has to be more effort exerted. There cannot exist the "throwing in the towel" option. The breakthrough or result you are searching for is normally just beyond doubt or fear. Hold on a little while longer, and push through while pulling away from people, places, or things that lead you astray from your intended purpose.

CHAPTER 9

Gaining Momentum Backward

CERTAIN CHANGES IN life can alter our sense of direction and bring about the whirlwind of confusion. These changes exist to get you going in diverse directions and ultimately hinder you from achieving greatness within. The coexistence of the failure and success mentality will only cause your progress to be stagnant.

The art of deception will only minimize the pain for a moment, but when reality hits, you will still be in the same place as before. Time is the only thing that will change.

Have you ever witnessed an individual who is stuck in his or her ways? Every time you meet them, it's the same story as before. Nothing changes but their age, and they embrace this stagnation as the truth. They hold on to past victories as well as failures and rarely desire to achieve anything greater than what they have already achieved.

This state of mind should be recognized as settlement because no matter what the situation is, the only way out is to just settle rather than fight for what matters the most—purposeful living! Many individuals settle in life due to the backward movement of their process. Every time they reach a milestone, there is a temporary setback. They have a home, but the water pipe breaks. They have a car, but the engine blows. They have a family, but divorce separates that. They have riches, but depression is their mate. They have fame, but everyone is attached just for the fame. They have won the championship, but a car accident leaves them unable to play the next year. These stories can go on forever. Just fit your situation into the setting, and you will realize it's a part of life.

Once we grasp the fact that life happens, we understand that it's how we respond to what happens that will determine how successful we become. It is always easier to respond negatively and blame others for where you are in life, but a face-to-face encounter with the self will always bring forth the truth when you stare yourself in the eyes long enough. Many individuals glance at themselves momentarily without ever coming to grips with the situation at hand.

The book of James chapter 1 verse 23–24 describes an individual who "beholdeth himself, and goeth his way, and straightway forgetteth what manner of man he was." The Weymouth New Testament version sheds light with this translation: "Although he has looked carefully at himself, he goes away, and has immediately forgotten the sort of man he is". These verses refer to a person who hears proper instruction or constructive criticism and momentarily says they will do better but produces the opposite results as if they never received any kind of instructions. This type of behavior will only lead to a wilderness mentality and a froward process rather than a forward progress.

When will there be a change? It will all lie in the hands of the individual. Although life has dealt us a hand full of setbacks, we have to develop a strategy of how to play the hand and not worry about the cards or situation in another person's hand. Our minds have to be fixed on the end result or purpose rather than take the narrow-minded approach of "It's just the way things are for me." Please cancel all the pity-party invitations and send out some belief statements with "Paid in full with confidence" stamped on them! It all starts and ends with your belief, so take a look in the mirror and decide to believe!

CHAPTER 10

Such a Time as This!

W HY NOW? AT this junction in life, why is this dilemma facing me? Thank you for asking. "For many are called, but few are chosen" (Matthew 22:14). In all walks of life, there must exist someone cut from a different cloth to bring about change or orchestrate a movement that empowers others to succeed. Many people are called upon to do certain things or perform tasks specifically designed for them, but there are a handful of individuals who are chosen for a greater cause. Who knows whether you have been chosen for such a time as this?

The situation may seem unbearable, and there is no light in this dark place. But if you can within the moment express gratitude and humility, the answer lies ahead. You must seek to embrace the trial rather than attempt to avoid it.

In the first book of Samuel chapter 16:1–23, a monumental moment takes place in the life of several individuals who were affected by being called versus being chosen.

Prior to this story, the current leader was rejected and basically removed from operating in a position of authority. King Saul had been chosen by the people to become king, but not specifically by God. The people pleaded with the prophet to find them a king due to the fact that other nations had kings. They wanted to fit in and be a part of the popular crowd instead of waiting on destined leadership. The behavioral patterns of the people's chosen leader would be revealed in time.

In 1 Samuel 8:10–18, Samuel warned the people of the pending behaviors:

- He will take your sons and appoint them for his own chariots and to be his horsemen, and some will run before his chariots.

- He will appoint captains over his thousands and captains over his fifties.
- He will set some to plow his ground and reap his harvest, and some will make his weapons of war and equipment for his chariots.
- He will take your daughters to be perfumers, cooks, and bakers.
- He will take the best of your fields, your vineyards, and your olive groves and give them to his servants.
- He will take a tenth of your grain and your vintage and give it to his officers and servants.
- He will take your male servants, your female servants, your finest young men, and your donkeys and put them to his work.
- He will take a tenth of your sheep, and you will be his servants.

After all this, Samuel lets them know what their response would be to this type of leadership. "And you will cry out in that day because of your king whom you have chosen for yourselves, and the Lord will not hear you in that day" (verse 18).

Regardless of the warnings and many disasters that awaited the people, "nevertheless the people refused to obey the voice of Samuel; and they said, No, but we will have a king over us, that we also may be like all the nations, and that our king may judge us and go out before us and fight our battles" (verse 19).

"So the Lord said to Samuel, 'Heed their voice, and make them a king'" (verse 22).

The behaviors of individuals who are chosen by people versus by God are in direct conflict of what leadership looks like. Called leaders normally have good intentions, but most of their decisions are based on their own agendas. In every warning Samuel gave the people about Saul it was mentioned how he would take from others for his personal gain. He would use others to promote his own agenda. The things you have worked so hard for, he would take for himself. The individuals closely connected to you—from your children, coworkers, and community—will also be affected by this type of leadership. Called individuals can easily get caught up in the self, demonstrating prideful ways and making the priority of those assisting them less important. Your earnings will be affected as well. It will seem as if the more you make, the less you bring home due to the corruption of the metric system that is set up within this type of leadership. The rise and fall of people- or popularity-chosen leaders is laid out in 1 Samuel chapter 8 through 30.

In chapter 16, there is the rise of new leadership chosen by God instead of by people. Destined leaders have defining behaviors that are revealed in their humility and desire to empower others. They focus on the message over the method and seek to be examples rather than self-exalters of their own agenda.

Maybe you are telling yourself, "I am no leader based on my height, my appearance, my intellect, my color, my race, my ethnicity, etc." We can come up with all types of reasons why we feel we are undeserving to lead. The world or people judge leaders based on the outward appearance, but God chooses leaders based on their hearts.

In the book of Samuel chapter 16, God instructed Samuel to go to Jesse the Bethlehemite, and there he would find the king he had chosen to lead the nation.

When Samuel arrived, he consecrated Jesse and his sons and invited them to the sacrifice or place of transition.

Eliab was the first son, who appeared before Samuel, and according to his appearance, Samuel assumed this was the chosen leader. But God said, "Do not look at his appearance or at his physical stature, because I have refused him. For the Lord does not see as man sees; for man looks at the outward appearance, but the Lord looks at the heart" (1 Samuel 16:7 Amplified Bible [AMP]).

Abinadab passed by next but was not chosen.

Shammah passed by next but was not chosen.

Jesse made seven of his sons pass by, and God chose none.

> And Samuel said to Jesse, "Are all the young men here?"
> Then he said, "There remains yet the youngest, and there he is, keeping the sheep."

And Samuel said to Jesse, "Send and bring him. For we will not sit down till he comes here." (1 Samuel 16:11 New King James Version [NKJV])

The Bible describes the youngest son as ruddy, with bright eyes, and good-looking.

And the Lord said, Arise, anoint him; for this is the one! (1 Samuel 16:13)

You can notice a clear distinction between the other brothers versus David.

The brothers were consecrated or dedicated for a religious purpose. They had invitations to the sacrifice or place of transition. Their appearance seemed to qualify them for the leadership position. The prophet even thought they were qualified—meaning, people with the vision can make errors in choosing leadership if they don't have a keen sense of hearing and awareness. Their father had his favorites. Leaders or fathers who choose to mentor the next generation without guidance from God will ultimately make the wrong choice based on favoritism and partiality. The father also was making the choice based on his sons' ages.

In regard to David, he was never given an invitation to the place of transition. He wasn't consecrated like his father and older brothers; instead, he was anointed or chosen officially to do an important job and was also chosen by divine intervention. It took God to speak to Samuel and let him know what was going on in this season. One leader was being rejected while another was being raised.

While Saul was busy rebelling against God, David was busy keeping sheep. He wasn't worried about leading people. What he didn't know was that God had been developing his ministry through his workplace, which was in the field. A lot of individuals think they will achieve leadership status within the confines of religion, but they don't understand that the greatest opportunities lie within their field or workplace. David adapted skills of leadership from the sheep and also how to battle from protecting the sheep.

God saw David when those that were close to him looked away and ignored him. They did not have the ability to recognize the potential within David. When it comes to recognizing potential, it takes someone who is connected to your Creator, who has specifically set you apart for a specific work. You ultimately know when you are chosen when you take a look back at the process and the path laid out for this moment.

Social media has dubbed millions as leaders based on who has the most followers. The number of followers doesn't designate you as a chosen leader; it only means you're popular. When you have a bulk of followers based on the truth and transparency of reality, then you will realize what leadership is designed to be. It's not built on falsehood and fantasy but the internal integrity system God has already put in place. David's brothers were popular and appealed to the masses, but the leader chosen for "such a time as this" was after God's own heart.

The leader who is after God's own heart usually takes ownership of their mistakes. They love structure and order. Rules and guidelines already laid out by God are not altered to fit their lifestyle, but they adjust their lifestyle to God's law. They fall in line with the guiding principles to achieve success and avoid taking shortcuts or the easy way out. They don't allow others to influence their integrity, but they hold fast to the promises of God and patiently persevere through the process. Regardless of the situation or how giant the Goliath is, they trust solely in the name of the Lord because it is a strong tower and safe place for them. Quite frankly, to keep it simple, they are giant slayers!

CHAPTER 11

Who Am I Now?

(Jesus Came to Save *That* Which Was Lost)

MANY INDIVIDUALS, IF not all individuals, are constantly on a search for a purpose of existence. The many changes in lifestyle or behavior will be a constant reminder of the desire for meaning. "Why am I here?" and the cloudy inquiries of "Where do I go?" "What do I do?" "Why did I choose?" "How did I get here?" and "When is this cycle going to end?" are in motion to offer suggestive reasons but never provide true clarity. Without true clarity, individuals often wander off into a field of lies and misconceptions, which gradually leads them astray, like a sheep away from its shepherd.

> The Lord is my Shepherd; I shall not want. He maketh me to lie down in green pastures: he leadeth by the still waters. (Psalm 23:1–2)

The chaotic situations in our lives that affect us emotionally, physically, and mentally can be brought into balance when we are surrounded by "still waters." The mistake we often make is trying to make clear and concise decisions when we are surrounded by chaos. It helps when we can pull back from this tug and find an atmosphere of calmness. Our souls are wildly entangled with complicated relationships from baby-daddy drama, baby-mama drama, bad uncles, sassy sisters, bragging brothers, angry aunts, teenage deceptions, stepdaddies, stepmommas, false teachers, fake leaders, racism, judgmental systems, rape, incest, molestation, drugs, alcoholism, crime, injustice, polluted politics, miscarriages, abortions, homosexuality, lesbianism, gossiping, slandering, social media, video gaming, sports, gambling, etc. The list goes on and on. It can fill up an entire city if all the dysfunctional relationships are listed. Regardless of what the relationship is, our souls have to be restored. It takes time, but with the proper leadership in place, the process is bearable. It becomes overwhelming when we attempt to isolate ourselves and do it on our own.

In the above verse, the shepherd leads the sheep to the still waters. Still waters usually represent streams that flow calmly and peacefully, producing a serene atmosphere where an individual can think clearly as well as organize a structured thought process. The ability to have that thought process structured would open up channels to success and would grant the individual access to the tools needed to obtain that success.

The waters also provide a sense of refreshment and quenching thirst that has been brought on by a constant chasing after people, places, or material things. The pursuit of who we are as individuals can leave us empty and desiring to be fulfilled from all the wrong sources. It would take but a moment for us to consider the damage to our souls and seek to rectify the internal disarray by choosing consistent leadership who will provide us with the truth of who we really are.

The pivotal point in the transition of soul restoration is what type of shepherd or leadership we choose. Ultimately, when we decide to get our life in order or to fix our soul, there has to be some type of leader chosen. "No man is an island" (from a poem by John Donne). Therefore, it's necessary to search out instruction and guidance from individuals who are equipped with shepherd like characteristics. To achieve the optimum level of performance and to enhance your ability to overcome adversity, someone has to be able to sense the internal struggle. All the experiences within this war that you have endured, along with the intense trauma undergone, are keenly recognized by the wisdom and insight of a good shepherd.

Jesus says: "I am the Good Shepherd. The Good Shepherd puts the sheep before himself, sacrifices himself if necessary. A hired man is not a real shepherd. The sheep mean nothing to him. He sees a wolf come and runs for it, leaving the sheep to be ravaged and scattered by the wolf. He's only in it for the money. The sheep don't matter to him" (John 10:11–13 The Message [MSG]).

Regaining our identity through soul restoration will be truly successful when we allow the guidance of a leader who is not in it for the money, fortune, or fame but is solely there to witness the results of sacrificial leadership. This type of leadership leads from the bottom of the pyramid, or servant style, instead of at the top, shouting out commands, dictations, threats, and intimidations.

Some leaders choose to help you with identity issues through fear and want you to become a slave to their system. They capitalize on your weaknesses and build your hopes on falsehood. What they offer you is momentary satisfaction instead of destiny fulfillment. Good shepherds or leaders invest in the internal makeup of *you*. They are motivated to see you achieve victory within first and provide you with the necessary tools to shape the manifested success ahead. They will never leave you or forsake you, but they always exist in the ongoing process to build your life and legacy. This type of leadership not only helps you find true identity but also motivates you to help others find theirs.

CHAPTER 12

After This, Then What?

THE BEGINNING OF this war is intense with the constant progression of pain, stress, aggravation, turmoil, favoritism, partiality, etc. It may seem to last a lifetime when it's only for a short term. The reality is, there has to be a plan to move forward after surviving the vigorous labor within this war. In the midst of all that is going on, how can a plan be developed for sustainability? How will everything you have gone through work out as a support system for the successful future ahead? Every moment of survival and overcoming of obstacles eventually becomes a foundation to build your success on. The pivotal point will be your perception.

It can be very disappointing when the captain chooses another individual ahead of you and the anchor that you depend on fails. Substitutions can be a hindrance to the plans one has to pursue a successful life. The complication of spinning in the crossroads can lead an individual on a path of indecisiveness and result in a severe state of weakness. We fight to draw strength from the things or people we want or desire to keep moving forward, but at the same time, we begin to experience major setbacks. Our greatest downfall will become reality when we allow pride's invasion to sweep through our thinking process and overtake our decision-making skills.

We are constantly trying to establish a stronghold to continue in this tug-of-war and use various tools gathered from the war itself to reinforce our stance. It may seem like our small victories account for nothing because every time we make progress forward, there comes along a change that seems to set us back. So we try by gaining momentum *backward*.

The apostle Paul gives us a simple solution when he is trying to make strides forward to achieve his ultimate purpose. He says: "Brothers and sisters, I do not consider that I have made it my own yet; but one thing I do: forgetting what lies behind and reaching forward to what lies ahead" (Philippians 3:13 Amplified Bible [AMP]).

The difficulty of this challenge is being able to forget and reach simultaneously. Some individuals attempt to forget the past but fail to use the past events to assist with their reach forward. Their confidence level has been consumed by what lies behind, and the clear vision of what lies ahead is tenuous. When we get back to the basics of who we are and understand our purpose, we will get clarity of what lies ahead. We will remove the limits of our belief system and continue to move forward in spite of the circumstances around us. No matter what we are confronted with in life, our focus will remain on the end result instead of the present crisis. Although the intensity of the tug-of-war has a tendency to increase, the fixation of our purpose and destiny will make us resilient and able to adjust and align ourselves with the predestination of our existence. What lies ahead is already there, but being able to capitalize on it will be the differentiator between success and defeat.

Now that we have arrived at this junction in the war, after this (our past), then what (our future)? What's our response to the question at hand? Since we can't control the past, we have to use everything from it and incorporate it within our present process. If we can achieve this, then we can positively influence the path to our future.

There is greatness in you, so dig deep in this season and know that God has your back. He understands the tug and is ready to mold your accomplishments up to now into the most brilliant work ever. Be encouraged, be prepared, and be receptive to the overflow of blessings headed your way. It only takes one of God's blessings to change your life. The miracle in the blessing is that it comes through multiple windows. It's only one blessing, but there are multiple windows, which signify the size of the blessing and its ability to flow.

> Bring the full tithe into the storehouse, that there may
> be food in my house. And thereby put me to the test,

says the LORD of hosts, if I will not open the windows of heaven for you and pour down for you a blessing until there is no more need. (Malachi 3:10 English Standard Version [ESV])

The beginning of the scripture is the turning point of your life. The tithe that God is requiring is evidently not in the storehouse yet. There is a command to bring the full tithe into the storehouse. Obedience is going to be the key to your next level. Integrity will also be a key factor, as God says to bring the full tithe. Many individuals experience major setbacks because they withhold from God and give him partial instead of what he fully requires. We must not get confused about what a storehouse is. Many try to make the storehouse a church or religious organization, but if this were the case, would hunger exist? Selah.

God himself is pouring the blessing down through multiple windows of heaven with the sole purpose of eliminating the voids that the tug-of-war has created. There is much misunderstanding about tithing, giving, and finances when it comes to God. The benefit with understanding God's principles is, things always work in your favor. It's pretty simple with God; when you sow, you reap. The mistake many of us make is, we tend to sow into the wrong people, places, and things; therefore, we reap inconsistent things from those mistaken areas. Then we build our future on the inconsistent things we reap. Now we have an inconsistent, out-of-balance lifestyle, which will ultimately lead us right back into the same tug-of-war we emerged from. What we don't want to happen is for multiple tugs-of-war to break out in our lives that will eventually bring major destruction to our belief system.

After this tug-of-war, we must connect to mentors and chosen leaders who will be able to instruct us. We will need to seek out those with godly wisdom and understanding. Search for a storehouse to bring your tithe into so the blessing of God can overflow in your life. This overflow will enable you to assist others in eliminating voids, thus helping those with a lack of identity to regain that which was lost and to become productive individuals. The next movement in our nation will be running back to God because of the intensity of the tug-of-war individuals are involved in. Many will seek to understand the why, how, when, who, and what of their situations. Chosen leadership will be in place to receive those individuals who are on the brink of giving up and who are settled in the "all hope is gone" mindset.

The pull of this war will be supernatural and above comprehension, but the manifested results will show how mighty God is. It's time to hold your head up high and walk this season out victoriously. See you at the top!

> Wisdom is supreme—so acquire wisdom, and whatever you acquire, acquire understanding! (Proverbs 4:7 New English Translation [NET Bible])

CPSIA information can be obtained
at www.ICGtesting.com
Printed in the USA
LVOW08*1621280318
571475LV00008B/77/P